OLD MAN THINGS
— and —
MARE's TALES

Old horseman stories and thoughts from under a horse's tail

ELIZABETH WILEY MA JD, POMO ELDER

Order this book online at www.trafford.com
or email orders@trafford.com

Most Trafford titles are also available at major online book retailers.

 www.trafford.com

North America & international
toll-free: 844 688 6899 (USA & Canada)
fax: 812 355 4082

Our mission is to efficiently provide the world's finest, most comprehensive book publishing
service, enabling every author to experience success. To find out how to publish your book,
your way, and have it available worldwide, visit us online at www.trafford.com

ISBN: 978-1-6987-1033-4 (sc)
ISBN: 978-1-6987-1034-1 (e)

Print information available on the last page.

Trafford rev. 11/23/2021

INTRODUCTION

Over decades, no matter what we were doing, we found old people, people who told stories. People who volunteered and help students learn with those stories. Many times those old people knew a lot more than the teachers and Principals they were volunteering to help.

Little old people who volunteered at the zoo, or the pound or at animal rescues that could seem to talk to the animals, and help them recover from the loss of their homes, and whatever trauma they had suffered, from losing their homes, to abandonment, to death of owners they were always glad to pass along their quiet wisdom.

We recognized that some of the stories were not always truth, but we said, this is not a court case, and even court cases have a lot of big tall tales in them. Sometimes the tall tales taught more than the well thought out, researched and academically tried and reported as God's truth. So we added them to our teaching toolbox.

One of the husbands started to say these stories reminded him of old tales his Grandfather had told when all the kids were anywhere doing a project or just needing to be diverted from pestering "busy" adults. He called them, in Spanish "old man things". These could vary from how to take the parts of a broken toilet out and put in a new one, to anoint tales of how to make sure you caught a fish, and did not get bitten to death by mosquitoes while out fishing.

We decided to call the same tales from women, Mares Tales.

INTRODUCTION

Our books are written as on ongoing series for high risk youth, veterans, and first responders as well as their parents and those who are raising them.

One of the reasons for starting this series was we, as special needs teachers, as therapists, as Directors of programs and private schools for high risk youth began to recognize how many of the children and youth were children of veterans, grandchildren of veterans, and also first responders.

We then noticed the numbers of minority children and poverty level financial back grounds were the reality for high risk children and youth. We saw children of Mothers who had been as young as NINE at the birth of their child among the high risk students. Whether rich, or poverty level, we saw children of alcohol, sexual, and drug addictions.

We saw children as young as 18 months labeled with an alphabet of mental health disorders, medicated and put into "special schools" where in fact media found they were often warehoused, abused, and not taught at all. Upon seeing a news story about the schools discovered at some of the licensed sites, in which children and teens often did not have desks, or chairs to sit on, let alone proper educational supplies and equipment for special learning program, we joined with others, and designed programs.

We were naive enough to think our work, offered FREE in most cases, would be welcomed especially as we offer it free and often through research projects, but, it was NOT valued or wanted.

What? we asked?

We went back to college and while earning degrees we had apparently NOT needed while working with children of the very rich in expensive private schools, we did research projects to document our findings. To find ways to overcome the problems. Again, our work was NOT valued or wanted.

One of our associates, who had asked many of us to volunteer in a once a month FREE reading program in the local public schools, was held back for almost two years doing paperwork and proving her volunteers, most of them parents of successful children, teens and adults, could read a first five years book and teach parents how to read those books to their own children. She was a Deputy United States Prosecutor, and had recruited friends from all levels of law enforcement, child and family services, education and volunteer groups that served children and families.

None the less, we continued our work, met a fabulous and expensive Psychiatrist who was building his own server system and the first online education project after creating a massive and encompassing medical examination study guide for graduate medical students to assist them in passing global and national medical examinations for licensing.

We worked with a team of citizens and specialists in education who had created a 39 manual project for students, parents and teachers to be able to learn on their own.

This series of books includes ideas, history and thoughts from the students, the parents, and professionals who work with these situations.

Jesus was told, don't have children wasting your time, and he responded, let the children come.

Our work is to bring children to us, and to those who have the heart and love to develop the uniqueness and individuality of each of God's creations. Many of them are of different religions, and beliefs, and many are atheists but believe fully in the wonder and uniqueness of every human.

To all who have helped and continue to help children and anyone wanting to learn, we thank God and we thank you.

CHAPTER ONE

Old people DO know things:

We, as a nation, as a world, have gotten the idea that new is all that matters.

In those wise words of Dr. Phil, "how is that working for you".

In the movie "Monster in law" the new trend in talk show guests and the young woman taking her job push the talk show host over the edge.

In real life, we hear news reporters telling us so called news as if it is a trendy new drink commercial. Watch and old news person in a clip, and compare it to most news of today. The police pursuits that take over the entire news, who wants to watch them, give a 30 to 60 second review of it TOMORROW, except possible to say STAY OFF this or that freeway or roadway.

People run TO a fight. I teach students to LEAVE and tell an adult who is responsible for the safety of ALL the students. Our country and the world is in dire need of a few brains, just as that scene in "Monster in law" shows.

I have an excuse, I have severe brain injuries from a high fever disease and one too many concussions from being hit by drunk drivers. And yet, I find learning everything from walking and talking over a second time, I am doing pretty well compared to many people who are supposed to have quality educations.

I used to like to watch CSPAN because I enjoyed the legal arguments, and the consensus reached in Congressional hearings. Now, like the "monster in law" scene, the situation is like a really bad talk show.

CHAPTER TWO

and on the other hand.....

It is up to each of us to listen, give respect, and do some research if need be, to figure out what is best for our situation at this very moment. NOT what we THINK we want, but what some old person has bothered to take time out and tell us we might need to rethink, before getting ourselves in a big mess.

We are ALL born with an instinct to eat, walk, be loved, and love. We are NOT born with an instinct to do things that mean nothing in the long run.

We have been well taught to buy the "snake oil" we are sold several times an hour by commercials, ads in magazines, and even comments by our family and friends.

In other countries they may well be in need of revolution, BUT, as the Native Americans found out, the land grubbers and asset stealers, and slave makers will kill you to the last one if they can get away with it if you fight them. SO, you might have to eat the Rez cheese (the treaty foods given in return for stop standing up for yourself when in fact you are just going to be wiped out for saying get of four land) and figure it out, but today many Americans are cleaning nature, and recycling, and asking in some states, WHAT HAPPENED TO THE RECYLING, we pay for it, where is it. Some cities (truthfully, we did the research and ASKED the recycling regulations so expensive and time consuming the companies quit) wanted to force the best cans and bottles to be picked out by companies that bought them from the city picked up trash so the city could get the money that consumers are forced to pay at the check out for every single can or bottle.

MY Grandmother had to have separate cans for plastic, glass, aluminum, other metals, paper and cardboard, and was expected to compost anything that might be sticky or smelly or have one SMALL can for pick up at the curb for those items. Our city and county went backwards when the rest of the country was making recycling mandatory and doing a good job with it.

These are good things to discuss with old people, they know how it used to be, and how people got to the idea that filling the world, oceans, and lakes and polluting air, water and even dirt was not a good idea if we wanted a future for ourselves, let alone those who come after us.

One day, teaching an equine therapy three hour program, which might become THE ONLY positive program the first time offenders in a pre-probation project for probation, we overheard the girls talking about having a baby and getting their welfare check.

The regular lesson went on hold.

Patricia had a lesson for just this situation. These girls were average age 13!

She asked them about their dreams, what did they want in life, and then asked, do you think it will be easier to make those dreams come true with one or more babies, OR to work on your dreams, travel, go to college, or start a career in something you love, save, learn about finance and how to buy a house, and buy one, and THEN find someone who loves you for yourself,

NOT your things, and have a child or two, because you love and will take care of them, not because they will get you a welfare check.

Patricia has a way to get the girls thinking, and dreaming and making a commitment to themselves.

Part of this project, when we get more than the three hour program to get first offenders to make that commitment to themselves is to go through programs with banks, credit unions, and others who help young people begin to see it is NOT about what someone hands you, but what you build for yourself, instead of not doing anything because it was NOT handed to you.

CHAPTER THREE

DID you know?

There are things you do not know that you need to know, the reasons you need to know these things are as many as the things you need to know.

Did you ever ask your Grandmother what video games she played as a child? Did you ever ask your Grandfather about the school bus ride? Did you ever ask your elderly neighbor if their family had a refrigerator, a television, a phone (what kind?) running water? How about an indoor bathroom? A shower? With hot water?

Most of the greatest kings and rulers in the world did NOT have some of the things YOU can buy, even if you pick up cans and bottles and turn them in to save enough money to do those things.

Take a bus.

Look back in history.......until this last century a "bus" was a long wagon with seats, if in a "good" rich neighborhood it might have a cloth roof with fringe, and was pulled by a horse to team of horses.

Look at your phone and see what dates and time it is.

In the past even Kings did NOT have watches, certainly no cell phones. Until the past century it did little good to have one of the oldest phones, no one else had one, so there was no one to call. Only the past decade or so have we been able to purchase a phone that gave us the date, times and let most people receive talk, then text and now data on our watch, or cell phone.

Look online and see how some very famous and powerful people are believed to have passed away. Many of them passed from things that today are easily cured or prevented.

King Tut, the Boy Pharaoh, you can go to museums when the Tut exhibitions come through near you. OR you can find online and video history accounts of his life. MRI and other modern tests have shown he more than likely was hurt, either in battle, or in practice for battle, and died from an infection that today the mildest antibiotic would cure. It might be that an antiseptic spray anyone can purchase at a dollar store would have cleaned and killed the bacteria that many believe may have killed him.

Plays, most music, parades were only for the very rich and kings. Today we watch them on television, or listen to music on radio, or disc players.

Mozart could not just play music, he wrote it, both he and Beethoven, among many others, could hear music in their heads, and write the notes on paper for others to play perfectly. Mozart thought it was not OK that much of the beautiful music was forbidden to the people. Only the super rich and aristocrats could listen to it. He would attend musical or orchestral performances, and with his superior knowledge of music and writing music, come away and write every note for every piece of music he heard to find musicians, and perform them for the people.

There were dancers, and writers, among them William Shakespeare that wrote musicals, plays, and piece for musicians to play that no one was supposed to be allowed to hear, but the elite.

The American Founders, in the Constitution said NO ONE could ever create an elite in America, we know that this principle has not been kept by many people, but it is our duty to learn and live by those rules, to give others the rights, we ourselves want. In many other countries, there are NO rights. The people are under the demands and rules, often with death penalties or long prison sentences to try and live free.

CHAPTER FOUR

MAIL, *packages, cards*

*W*hile there has been mail for some centuries, and even in ancient kingdoms there were people who ran, or rode a horse to deliver these things to kings and the richest of citizens, most of the people either did know know how to read, or in certain areas were not allowed to read.

As you learn about history, you will find that even some religions refused to allow ALL the people learn to read or write. The elite did NOT want them to gain power by learning, and by communicating by writing to one another. WOMEN were in many countries, and many religions not allowed to read, or write. Men in those nations, or religions wanted to have more power than they could have if EVERYONE had the right to read and write.

Today, thanks to satellite science and the international space station and the research needed to develop the communication systems from earth to space vehicles and stations, we ALL can tap a few words, or letters, click our cell phone and in moments we have a response from someone around the world. Many of the most undeveloped countries have at least ONE cell phone in town that the mayor can use to ask for help, or know what is going on in the world.

In the seventies three healers, from Native American nations, that due to being pushed together by the westward genocide, had been enemies for many decades, centuries, went to many healing meetings around the Americas, they met with Congress, and spoke to the UN general meeting to try and warn and persuade the people of earth to honor our Creator and save the plants, animals, air, water and even the ocean and dirt from the greedy destruction for financial gain by a few.

These old men told of a Native American Healer, honored by all three nations, who had painted a prophecy on a buffalo hide that had been tanned silvery white. They brought this buffalo hide and/or copies of it to many around the world. By 1970, the technology existed to take a picture of the hide, and produce posters, and small pictures of the hide drawings for newspapers and magazines.

One of the items painted on the buffalo hide

was a giant web, a spider, her front feet on the web to feel movement as most spiders do as they watch their webs for something to be caught. The web was called "THE WORLD WIDE WEB" in those ancient Native American languages. The warning given three hundred years before was that one day this web would surround the world, it would be the choice of the PEOPLE to use it for evil, or to choose to use it to once and for all unite the PEOPLE of the world and give us lasting peace and we would care restore and care for the earth, the water, the air, and restore plenty and good harmony to the lands our Creator gifted us all with. Not just Native Americans, but all humans.

No one knew what it meant, could it be telegraph, could it be train tracks, could it be telephone??? Did it mean air travel?

The other drawing on the hide was the earth, the poles covered with ice melting as a huge dragon spitting fire under the ice melted the glaciers that would drown the earth as the waters rose around the world.

Again, no one knew, how could they, three hundred years ago, or even in the early seventies that nuclear weapons would be tested using submarines under both poles. The submarines that do this type of testing often are painted by the sailors with fiery faces of dragons, AND the weapons not only melt the ice, the water temperature below is raising so the sea life is dying out. From the tiny plankton to the hugest of whales, polar bears, walrus and other northern sea creatures can NOT live with their food chains broken and with the horrifying radiation.

Read online: there are articles about the finding of "dead water" zones, that are mainly blamed on leaks from nuclear plants, or "accidents" of some type of nuclear weapon.

In the fifties, during the big nuclear war threats, the scientists began to warn humans that radiation from these bombs would last a minimum of 69 years. The war mongers were bragging they had enough "fire power" to kill every living thing, NOT just humans, 70 times over. I was a small child when my Mom had no sitter and took us to a seminar at Cal Tech, headed by a General to find out how we could make our city prepared, and be prepared for "nuclear winter" should a nuclear war happen.

We already had a drill once every month when all school children and employees of big companies cowered under desks until the alarm rang a tone to tell us to go to the bomb shelters.

The shelters, depending on how educated and rich the parents of the students were (these were public schools, but segregated by race and financial holdings of parents we found years later) had water in sealed barrels, and food for "crisis".

The General kindly told the people at that seminar that we were the lucky ones, with Cal Tech, JPL and budding NASA (NASA itself came in the next decade, after its start in 1958 in Houston) would be first strike, full strike targets in a nuclear war. We would be gone in a flash, more than likely never seeing or hearing anything. Just dust.

Then he proceeded to tell the PEOPLE that if they did manage to live in a community outside that first strike perimeter, the nuclear radiation and waste would swirl around, in the winds and the force of the initial strike. He was kind enough to note that the huge nuclear silos, filled with atomic missiles we had seen brought in and loaded into the mountain would be hit by a first strike, and add to the nuclear power, radiation and waste of that first strike.

So much for second strike theory.

AND PEOPLE called those scientists and others "soft" and "communists" and "socialists" because they said it was time for humans to get it, war was obsolete, and it was time for lasting world peace and equality.

How did an ancient healer, from a confederacy of nations that had treaties for peace with thousands of small nations massed into one confederacy know this?

Read about Benjamin Franklin's research and living with the Native Nations in those confederacies to find out how they had worked out a system of self-governances, rather than kings, and others who had not worked out for the general person.

There is a new study, and documentary from Stanford archeology one this subject regarding the east coast nations and "the peacemaker". PBS "Native America" series has these in their archives and can be streamed.

CHAPTER FIVE

Medicine, Paramedics, Fire Departments, Police Departments, Protective military and NO draft

Look up all of these online: you are going to wonder how anyone lived, or got along.

While there are many Native medicines that today are being researched and used again as safer methods than some chemical only medications, we also want to explore if we are too ready to take a pill, or shot, or surgery to cure something that plants, herbs, food sources might cure just as easily, less expensively, and with less side effects.

DO some research before popping something in your body. ASK your doctor. AND shock to say this, do not TELL your doctor that you saw a commercial that said you could get a medication because you "go to sleep at night" and "wake up in the morning" as some comedians love to point out, with only fifty-three after effects that include cancer, and even death.

Even when your doctor suggests medications to you, ASK and then do some research on your own about that medication. Sometimes the risk is worth the cure. Other times, it is not. YOU may have allergies that make that medication NOT the best one for YOU.

SHOCKING truth, you do NOT need pills, shots, or street drugs because you think you have a pain..... Most pain is a warning by your body to stop and pay attention to that area. This is the time to ask your DOCTOR, not listen to television commercials, what might be causing the pain. Many people take their own pain treatments, and find out way too late for a cure that they have a tumor, an infection, or other medical issue that once was able to be treated and cured easily and now may cost them their lives because it was NOT treated.

Many problems are treated by a change in diet, and more or different exercise. ASK your doctor. In the old days, if you talk to old people, there were people with cures for just about everything, they went about in trucks, or before that in horse drawn wagons, selling what came to be known as "snake oil" cures.

They did not work. Some did not harm you, but others did. Some could kill people with allergies, or weakened systems.

ASK your doctor.

In this past one hundred years there were few police, fewer fire persons, most of the fire department was volunteers who asked the town to help them raise money to buy equipment.

In the fifties, after the war, some cities began to add medical students in station wagons to pick up injured or ill persons and take them to the hospital.

Over time call boxes (no cell phones yet) to report emergencies and EMT services started to become part of every city, although some were still volunteer only and the emergency rooms were small two room buildings put on land donated by citizens, and built with funds raised by citizens. Doctors donated their time, in rotations, many of them because they were tired of just their clinic of runny noses and flu cases. Many of those doctors had been MASH doctors in the military during Korea, and Vietnam, Laos, and Cambodia. They knew how to run an emergency clinic in just a tent, let alone a small building with its own small operating room for setting bones, and stitching cuts.

Today, Doctors Without Borders, and SMILE and other medical teams go into third world undeveloped areas where they work as they can in limited working conditions. ALL of us can help them raise money, and work with groups such as Habitat for Humanity, or Rebuilding Together to get volunteers, donated, or discounted supplies and at least have a two room emergency set up for them.

Many doctors in rural places operate on a tarp, on the ground, in the spotlights of their offload vehicles. Many are now raising their own money when at home in their own practice to buy generators and operating lights, and bring their own sterile tools with them, taking them back to hospitals that will allow them to sterilize them.

There are many ways we can ALL work and donate to help build a better system around thee world.

The military hospital ships were loaned to large cities around America during Covid. Many military groups were put into active duty to take supplies and medicines to other nations to help their people. We can ALL work on projects that will build on that togetherness of the world.

The Constitution says that Americans have a right to decide to pay for, or provide young people to fight any war. The draft was used during World War I, World War II, and Korea, and all other wars until the people in the mid-sixties realized their young men were being drafted in their last year of high school, sent to boot camp, and in many cases gone to war before their first college course could begin in the fall.

People say many things.....but the Constitution says America has a new system, it is NOT run by an elite, and it can NOT be used for "empire" building in any way.

Many other people said, I am not going to raise my sons just to get drafted and be killed, maimed, or mentally destroyed before they are old enough to drink a beer legally. Look online and study those days, the draft is still there today, but limited to a time when Congress "might" decide it has to be reactivated for some "crisis" to defend our own country, NOT go into other countries to decide one side or the other of civil wars, or revolutions to throw outside business people out who are taking all the land, and assets, and impoverishing the people who own those elands and have tradition and history there for thousands of years.

ALL of these are human problems. ALL of them can and need to be human resolved, each country has to resolve the problems in their own way.

CHAPTER SIX

Street drugs, and other locker room myths.

Whether old men, or old women ASK them about these things.......none of this is trendy young people new ideas. Drugs and sex trafficking are OLD as the hills, OLD as the mountains and have never been for anything except to get young stooges to spend their money on ruining their lives.

I have spent much of my adult career working with gangsters. REAL gangsters do NOT use drugs, or get messed up with people who are likely to have brothers or fathers that will shoot them, or reduce the size of their sexual organs by six or eight inches.....and those old locker room stories are not true.......read up in medical books.

This is a rude chapter, plain spoken. When I was in college there was ONE guy who had more than eight inches when fully excited, AND everyone knew.....called him the telephone pole, and would NOT go out with him. He was a nice guy, some of us were honest about our reluctant attitudes toward this overgrowth. BUT the locker room stories continue, generation after generation causing men to feel inadequate.....and to kill animals, and sharks, to try and be the sexual heroes they hear about in the locker room.

ONE THING IS TRUE. There are medications that do help men who cannot have sex as much as other men in the locker room say they do, and there is NO reason in the world for men to buy expensive potions and powders made of rhino horn, elephant tusk, tiger or lion glands, or shark fin. The scientists have proven that if everyone cut their fingernails and toe nails, and threw it in collection boxes, it would be exactly the same as the animal parts that do NOT work. See a doctor, get a prescription and know one thing..........the last thing honest women want is to see a penis poked out at them for four hours.

There was one basketball player who used to brag that he had sex with over 2000 women in a short period of his career. WHAT we women wanted to know, was wrong with him that no one would have sex with him more than once. We decided to figure out if it could possibly be true. We ASKED the coach of the basketball team for the practice and play rules and regulations. Then we looked at a calendar and with games, practice, and lock downs, this man was a great big liar. OR he spent every free moment lying on the ground, penis held rigid with a sick or something, and had women run by and squat on him for their 15 seconds. That was THE ONLY way he could have had sex with that many women in that time frame.

WHERE THERE, we wondered, that many stupid women, who would take off their pants, and run by and squat on some guy they did not know........ the thought, over the years has been discussed, and the answers are always hell no.

We also, not wanting to get into a law suit with the porn industry wondered.....and found out that not one woman we asked thought the sex portrayed in porn is what she felt was intimate contact that she would want.

We felt, in classes that discussed this thought, that in fact, porn is for beat off teenage boys who are not ready for real sex, and dirty old men who no one is prepared to have sex with if she has a brain in her head. (or his head in these gender equality days). WHY we wanted to know, is this called ADULT, when in fact it is juvenile, immature, unrealistic, and self-entertaining for men (or women) who have never bothered to build a good sexual relationship for themselves, so have to resort to porn.

One day a young friend called me, crying. her husband had put up a pin up in their house. I said, OH, do not cry, and we called a gay couple we knew and went to visit them. They said, OH YES, we have just what you need, and gave her a picture of a guy so sexy no one could ever live up to it. She put it up over the top of the headboard of their bed. Her husband said, OK, OK, I get it.

Somehow we have gotten ourselves into a fake lifestyle that just is not real. People who are addicted to weird sex, especially men, are told, oh it is natural men think of sex every few seconds. If that is so, how come all movies and most books about husbands and wives, it is the husband out bowling, or playing golf, and NOT wanting to have sex as much as the wife.

My Dad was kind enough to tell all of us, if sex was really so much of a much, everyone would get married at 12, and f)(*k themselves to death before 13, so no kids, and humans would be over with. He said, sex is about

TWO people and they have to discuss it, and make it what they want it. DO NOT marry someone until you know what THEY are about.

Over life, this becomes very clear. People marry "virgins" and then are angry because the person is "cold" or "frigid".

Wee fail to teach people about sexuality. Sex, in scientific terms is a sperm and egg....when they merge, it is a new life. SOMEONE is responsible for that new life. It needs to be the two people who put those halves into a whole and start that life.

Abortion: In a class, we studied myths, one lady studied abortion and birth control. NEITHER was immoral until the church realized that as people got to know where those kids came from, they started using birth control or had abortions and there were no left over kids to give to the church for servants (slaves) or soldiers (more slaves) and most of those gifted children were not treated well. Young boys with good voices were gelded to keep their voices high longer for the enjoyment of the choir loving people. No one cared that those gelded kids had NO chance at a marriage and children.

Today we have sex education, not religious or secular, scientific and religious BOTH say if you cause a human to result, YOU need to take responsible and humane care of that human.

SOME states agree, IF you have a child, you do not have to marry, but BOTH parents will pay half of all money the taxpayers spend to support the child. BOTH parents are expected to get an education and a job and care for their child. Children that are taken away for abuse are taken care of, and BOTH parents pay child support to the State.

Young people need to understand, you do what you want, BUT today we have DNA and you are going to support your child. Those two or three million dollar premie care units per child, both parents better get a great education and a better job to pay those bills off.

Many families came from other countries and thought, WOW this house is big enough for ten families. They came from living in one room, and having ten or more children. The taxpayers in those areas said, OH NO, many of us do not even have one child, and we are not going to pay taxes for as many as 100 kids from one mansion to go to school.

People seem to have gotten the idea that America is a super rich country that can afford to support everyone else. The welfare is for those who are ill, old, need a hand to get through school and raise children alone, NOT for those who do not have a dream, do not want to work.

While volunteering my time in a community legal. clinic as a community mediator, I had to deal with a lot of the issues of families being evicted from poverty housing units. Many of the seniors were being evicted because their children and grandchildren were coming back and mooching off of them.

One young woman came in and wanted help for her mother, she had been evicted. In these city units there was NO excuse or defense against certain violations of the leases. One was brining gang members, or other criminals, and people who raced in the driveways and parking lots, or were convicted of stealing from the other tenants.

Her brother had done ALL of these things since quitting high school. This young woman was very well dressed. When I was leaving I just happened to see her parked near my truck. She was driving a new trendy vehicle at least a $100,000 vehicle. I am generally easy going, so said to her, how come you don't buy your Mom a house. She and I got into a conversation about *the fact that the poverty housing was for people who were not ever going to recover from illness or injury and for single parents who needed a hand for a time to go to school, and get a job, or plan for a business. She and other of her siblings had done very well, I said, buy your Mom a house, she had to sell her self-respect and dreams to keep a roof over your head, and a place for you to build and meet your dreams.*

AND, have a talk with your brother, he either goes back to school, stays away from criminals, or does not get to know where you all live. The new neighbors are not going to be any happier to have him, and his freeloading friends stealing from them then the people in the project are.

She understood two things that day, her Mom had let her son put the family out in the street, and that she could, and needed to protect her Mom from a disrespectful son who did not care if he got her evicted. These type of units were city funded, city owned, and the PEOPLE who lived in the units had created the rules so they were not just living in hell at the taxpayers expense.

CHAPTER SEVEN

"winning"

One day some doctors were sitting around the ER with nothing to do. One of them said, you know, I thought when I was a doctor, my whole life was going to be heaven on earth. Instead, I am the same guy, with the same problems, and now I also am responsible for life and death of other people.

That led to a discussion of how many of them had the same delusion, and earlier in life had thought when they got trophies, or scholastic awards, or even "the" popular girls as girl friends and wives......they STILL had the same themselves and problems they had before. Many of these doctors were now in therapy to help them figure out what was missing before, and how to resolve those problems before it cost a patient their life.

"winning" we have all heard that statement, "cheaters never win". We all see cheaters "winning" everywhere we go. One day I was talking to my Dad and he said, if you do your best, you know you did your best, and if someone cheated you out of a trophy, or ribbon, or even school slot, YOU know you did your best. THEY know that one day someone is going to discover the cheating.

I finally saw what that old saying meant.

In reality some people get things, STEAL things from others by their cheating, but they are cheaters, and stealers, NOT their best and they know it. They are often aware that other people know it as well.

During the days of affirmative action many very white people began to have Latin last names, and claimed to be Black, or Native American. Many Asians with solid background educations claimed to be minorities and took more slots in the minority jobs, and college spaces that were there to give an equalization of opportunity to many who did not have them in the past. One of my sisters was working for the accounting and review department of a huge county. She said, there are a lot more Native Americans than there should be. Being Native American she asked for proof of Native American background, not necessarily an enrollment in a BIA recognized Native Nation, but more than someone who suddenly started wearing bead earrings, and/or vest made of leather. Out of over 5,000 employees who had jobs with affirmative action status as Native American, less than ten had ANY proof of being Native American, or had even attended a Native Cultural event ever. Today we have DNA, but no more affirmative action. Many people who claim certain historical background on DNA checks do NOT have that background at all.

Another country decided to put in laws that forced everyone to prove their ethnic background, or be thrown out of the country they had grown up in, or been part of the founding groups left after no refugee camps or nations would take them. One of the major groups was Black, and when the DNA was taken, the Black citizens had more relationship to the ethnic historical persons than most of those who were coming in from big countries they did not want to pay taxes any longer...

The UN has in its Constitution the right of every human on earth to have a place to belong, meaning a nation of origin. This was supposed to mean just that. Instead fifty years later, the UN rights are no longer taught to students along with the responsibilities and native people are being thrown out, or financed out of their own countries.

CHAPTER EIGHT

Make sure you can care for yourself in a crisis

This past year plus, the Covid 19 has brought 188 countries to their knees, another nine refuse to admit they had any problem at all.

Yet some people STILL refuse to get their vaccinations, even with their own doctors having had the vaccines, and telling them to get the vaccines. And to keep them up as directed as research continues on this virus.

Whether a natural disaster, or vehicle accident, or becoming the victim of a crime....PEOPLE are NOT prepared for what life throws at them.

Many people seem to think that God, those that believe in God, is a vending machine. Put in prayer, get what you want, need, or miracles you forgot to think about.

While I personally believe in God, I know that God is not a vending machine, or lottery ticket machine.

Go to a yard sale, buy an old Scout, or Campfire, or Pathfinder book. These programs were never intended to be $16 a year free babysitting for your kids. They were started by people who wanted to help people left out by society learn how to survive, how to thrive.

People say, OH the kids are molested. IF YOU are there with them, they are NOT molested, and today the programs are on line. Unless computers have come a very bad long way, you child is safe on the protected online classes, and YOU can learn right along with them.

The subject of children taking care of adults is a tough one, and causes many psychological and social problems for children and teens. Learn to take care of all the realities and responsibilities of having a family BEFORE having children. Learn to speak the business language so your children are NOT doing the business or taking the responsibility of your family because you do not speak business American.

We call the language spoken in America, Business American. English is a language forced on the Native Americans, often by sending bounty hunters to round up the children, treating them worse than cattle on ranch round ups to take them to slaughter. The ranchers were out there to make sure the cattle were not injured or killed before getting them to slaughter and getting paid for them Dead or alive was the chant of the bounty hunters. The scalps of men, women and children were turned in along with the kids left alive enough to go to the BIA schools.

Business American has many words from the languages here, and brought here over the centuries, as well as new words created by advertising agencies to sell products. One day, we may have American Business dictionaries in books and online.

People talk about diversity, and believe they are talking about equality. Diversity is like putting everything in your refrigerator and cabinets into a blender and pushing blend.

Equality, with bicultural development is like a huge potluck table, or a salad bar. American Business language is that potluck, or salad bar of language.

After thirty or more years of ebonics being recognized, America has honored ALL Americans and how they speak, but the dictionary has not caught up. This means that while paying lip service (sorry for the pun)to language equality, those taking tests, and writing essays are crippled if they have not been taught APA and other forms of formal writing since middle school.

CHAPTER NINE

Love, relationships, sex

ASK old people. Most old people do NOT believe in old romance novels written by old maids who wrote them and sold them to young women who either married romantically and were trying to make the dream of romance stay alive by buying and reading those books instead of working on their real relationship.

Many others have married, and according to ancient Biblical regulations live in abusive, mentally stressing relationships because one day they might get left out of "heaven" if they are honest and get a divorce.

IF YOU have married a toad, admit it, get rid of that toad, spend a few years figuring out what YOU missed to get that toad, and then how to find a real love in your life.

NO ONE, say OLD PEOPLE, has a soul mate. It is like saying you found the herbal fountain of youth.....when in fact, you are going to get O LD. You can get plastic surgery until that little mark on your forehead is your belly button, you can buy thousands of dollars of make up or cleansers, but you are still going to get old. This is NOT to say do not spend time and money taking care of yourself. It is to say that when you are confident, and have lived every moment, and know each wrinkle and the smiles and tears that brought it.......THEN you are no longer afraid of being OLD, or even, shockingly, passing away one day. We all pass away someday.

John Lennon wrote and sang a song "Grow Old With Me". I think it is what marriage is supposed to be about. Marriage is not about some one with time and youth to make money to spend on make up, clothing and doing things to make themselves and YOU feel thrilled and fifteen forever.

"Grow Old With Me" is knowing that old fart or fart-ess is NEVER going to stop throwing their dirty socks on the floor. You either force them to hire *a maid, or you just pick them up, BUT you get some of your "flaws" forgiven as well.*

One woman managed to get to work, through college, and not fired for her wrinkled appearance, no one noticed. BUT when she got married, and the honeymoon began to fade, her spouse said she did not know how to wash clothing, or to fold it properly. HE was perfectly willing to do the laundry for the family the rest of their lives if he did not have to wear shirts folded to have a crease in the chest area, or a slightly reddish tint to most of the clothing as she forgot to properly separate the clothing before putting it in the washer.

They lived on in peace and love until she passed away from cancer years later, with no fights, no wrinkles, and no pinkish clothing.

Her secret was most of her clothing went to the cleaners, being high end suits needed for her job.

A marriage is to me, that "Grow Old With Me"....to in this insane, and chaotic world have one person who accepts you for all your flaws, as they become known, and all the wrinkles and slowing down as you both age.

A marriage is to me, making sure you both stay in love enough to take care of YOURSELF, not look at the other person and criticize them, because happiness would be yours, if THEY would just not be so wrinkly, or round (should have looked at the pictures of Mom and Grandmother in the family albums if you wanted skinny Minnie forever) or after retiring went back to clunking around the garage and coming in greasy and smiling from working on a vehicle that was never going to run for more than a day or two at best. Or invited friends over to play cards, or eat take out and gossip. (Men this does mean you as well, put a few beers, a pizza, and some men together, with cards, or an engine to work on, no group of women can ever equal the gossip going on).

CHAPTER TEN

Its All Too Much

YOU can make a difference in the world, ecology, environment, ending pollution, a world that saves wild lands, and wild animals

YOU can save lives, make smiles, make your own life happy and filled with joy.

The more you learn how to create dreams, find out how to accomplish them, and divide this into steps and take those steps, one at a time, the more of your dreams you will accomplish.

WHAT DO YOU WANT:

Write it down here.

Most people say they want more money. They want to win the lottery. They go buy a lottery or scratcher ticket. WHEN they win $5, they are mad, or disappointed. If you said win the lottery, why are you upset, YOU are the one who did not put an amount on how much you won, or when.

One day the liquor store near our house sold a lottery ticket. It was a huge amount at that time, almost $100 Million. No one showed up to claim the winnings.

We started to make up stories. We all bought our tickets there, most of us quick picks. We said, OH what's her name went to the Laundromat, what if she forgot that ticket was in her pocket and it was just mushy paper balls and she threw them away as she put her clothes from washer to dryer.

What if what's his name stepped out of his truck, and the ticket blew out of the ashtray where he leaves them, and he did not notice, and then it stuck to his boot. When he got in the house he just wore that ticket out while doing chores and cooking dinner. He did not even notice the little pieces of paper as he swept.

Many of us in life buy that ticket, but do NOT expect to win. WE know that the statistics are millions to one that you will win. BUT, got to give it a chance. SO we buy the ticket.

What if we had a two fold plan. ONE, we would buy the ticket, keep it in a safe place. Make up our mind to check out the reality of the chance of winning, and not stop with buying a ticket. Our second plan would be a way to make that amount of money ourselves, just in case!

I tell myself that each of us spent $2 or whatever, and the person who won got a great gift from all of us. I pray that they do not do the usual lottery ticket winner foolishness. Forget they have to pay almost 45% in our state in taxes, and that is that. Spend the rest on a house that the taxes cannot be paid the next year. The person can not afford the up keep of the house. Buys a vehicle that is hundreds of thousands of dollars to buy, insure, and where are you going to keep it.........

A friend got a great job and bought an expensive car he had liked. He drove to show it to some friends, his old car had had NO problem with their driveway. The new car was lower to the ground and the sharp angle between the street and the driveway tore the muffler off the new car. Then he found out that the parts and labor were several times that of his old car. He also found that the insurance on a car with that huge of a car payment was higher than his paid off vehicle.

Just an air filter on the mandatory oil changes and maintenance was more than he had paid at the corner for a full oil change, new filter, and the mechanics were friends who told him if they felt he needed something checked at the dealer on his car.

This is NOT to discourage buying of lottery tickets, I buy them when the pot is big. I have a plan for when I win. I will see my lawyer, my bank, and invest in housing for single Moms and elderly and disabled so I can get the majority of my tax paid returned to build more housing for those I want to help be home owners in developments that are created for their best interest.

When I start making money on my investments, I will reinvest to keep my tax advantages, and I will buy myself a thing or three that I have not already bought for myself along the way.

I did research on inheriting, or winning money long ago to make sure I did the best with my money for myself, my family and to help others who need a hand.

I had the same plan for inheriting money.

What did YOU spend your stimulus money on. Many people bought lottery tickets, NOT one or two, or ten. The whole pot. AND they lost, or won back fifty or a hundred dollars. Many people bought their children dirt bikes, motorcycles, four-wheel desert vehicles that they will be paying off for years, IF they have a job fast when COVID restrictions are withdrawn. Otherwise, the vehicles will be repossessed. Some of the kids have died or been maimed riding those vehicles without proper supervision.

CHAPTER ELEVEN

Happily Ever After

The choice of path is yours, no matter what the reality of this moment may be.........

This is a little old lady story (Mare tale) that is true. I had had a rough week or two, I asked God for a sign, I believe I had just been told there was nothing more they could do for me, my cancer was now just wait and die. They told me, go see your lawyer, don't make another appointment, you won't be here in two weeks. OF COURSE not quite that shockingly flat spoken, but I got the message. They did actually say, no appointment needed, and go see your lawyer...maybe it was that clear.

I went to the church my family in Pasadena had gone to since moving there in 1915 or so. My Grandfather and Great Uncle had been masons, and actually built that church, a complete copy of a British church. It looked like a castle.

I had no idea that that very day a new interfaith laying on of hands healing service at noon had started be held there. I went in to pray, and was invited to the Chapel for the service.

I left church, feeling that I was going to miss my family, my work, and then realized I had a Foundation I had to make plans for, fast. I thought, I need a sign. I turned a corner, and there, leaning against a trash can, with many trash bags, and pink table cloths tied around party dishes, was a large sign. It read "happily ever after".

Not going to be like Bruce Almighty in the movie, I heeded the sign, and stopped and put it in my truck. I knew the woman who owned the house briefly, as a neighbor you wave to. I knew the sign was out for the collection, and that this woman would NOT mind if I collected it.

One day I had been driving up the mountain to feed the horses, and a blustery wind was blowing. I saw her rushing around to rescue her Christmas

Decorations from her fences, gates and shrubs. I stopped, and helped her chase them down, replace them and secure them.

Another day I saw her with her children trying to pick the great oranges from her trees. There used to be wonderful orange groves in that area, and the homes that still had the trees in their yards were very fortunate. The oranges were amazing and juicy. I stopped and suggested they could stand in my truck bed, and we all laughed and picked oranges, and of course I got some to take home for ME!

Happily Ever After.

I thought about that, and thanked God. I fed the horses up the mountain and when I got home, had a message from my Doctor that the USC/UCLA hopeless cancer research team had decided to take my case.

They said, we think we can give you one or two more years. I am now 16 years cancer free, and living happily ever after. I thank God and pray for all who have negative medical reports. I tell them, sometimes God does give us what we want. I wanted more time with my family, my horses, my work, all happily ever after.

CHAPTER TWELVE

Closing:

This book has been an introduction to things we can learn from older people. It has been an advisory (we hope) for young people and parents, to make sure that we all honor and respect each other.

To help us all learn that old and new create a great blend of each person, with their own experiences and outlooks, BUT to be careful, whether old or new, to leave behind anger, bitterness, and hate......and trendy living. It is wonderful to find things we like, to enjoy them but when we are just a stooge, working to buy the latest new thing, or the advertised most expensive thing, to make us feel OK about ourselves.....it is an addiction.

God bless.

This is Donald, found by one of the riders out on the trail with a brother kitten who only lived one day. Donald was named by my older son, Tim, and lived with us for many years

Other books in our programs

Closing and Other Books by Author and team

Closing:

All of our group of books, and workbooks contain some work pages, and/or suggestions for the reader, and those teaching these books to make notes, to go to computer, and libraries and ask others for information to help these projects work their best.

To utilize these to their fullest, make sure YOU model the increased thoughts and availability of more knowledge to anyone you share these books and workbooks with in classes, or community groups.

Magazines are, as noted in most of the books, a wonderful place to look for and find ongoing research and information. Online search engines often bring up new research in the areas, and newly published material.

We all have examples of how we learned and who it was that taught us.

One of the strangest lessons I have learned was walking to a shoot in downtown Los Angeles. The person who kindly told me to park my truck in Pasadena, and take the train had been unaware that the weekend busses did NOT run early in the morning when the crews had to be in to set up. That person, being just a participant, was going much later in the day, taking a taxi, and had no idea how often crews do NOT carry purses with credit cards, large amounts of cash, and have nowhere to carry those items, because the crew works hard, and fast during a set up and tear down and after the shoot are TIRED and not looking to have to find items that have been left around, or stolen.

As I walked, I had to travel through an area of Los Angeles that had become truly run down and many homeless were encamped about and sleeping on the sidewalks and in alleys. I saw a man, that having worked in an ER for many years I realized was DEAD. I used to have thoughts about people who did not notice people needing help, I thought, this poor man, this is probably the most peace he has had in a long time. I prayed for him and went off to my unwanted walk across town. As I walked, I thought about myself, was I just heartless, or was I truly thinking this was the only moment of peace this man had had for a long time and just leaving him to it. What good were upset neighbors, and police, fire trucks and ambulances going to do. He was calmly, eyes open, staring out at a world that had failed him while alive, why rush to disturb him now that nothing could be done.

I did make sure he was DEAD. He was, quite cold rigid.

I learned that day that it is best to do what a person needs, NOT what we need.

Learning is about introspection and grounding of material. Passing little tests on short term memory skills and not knowing what it all means is NOT education, or teaching.

As a high school student, in accelerated Math and Science programs, in which I received 4.0 grades consistently, I walked across a field, diagonally, and suddenly all that math and science made sense, it was not just exercises on paper I could throw answers back on paper, but I realized had NO clue as to what it all really meant.

OTHER BOOKS BY THIS AUTHOR, AND TEAM

Most, if not all, of these books are written at a fourth grade level. FIrst, the author is severely brain damaged from a high fever disease caused by a sample that came in the mail, without a warning that it had killed during test marketing. During the law suit, it was discovered that the corporation had known prior to mailing out ten million samples, WITHOUT warnings of disease and known deaths, and then NOT telling anyone after a large number of deaths around the world started. Second, the target audience is high risk youth, and young veterans, most with a poor education before signing into, or being drafted into the military as a hope Many of our veterans are Vietnam or WWII era.

Maybe those recruiting promises would come true. They would be trained, educated, and given chance for a home, and to protect our country and its principles. Watch the movies Platoon, and Born on the Fourth of July as well as the Oliver Stone series on history to find out how these dreams were meet.

DO NOT bother to write and tell us of grammar or spelling errors. We often wrote these books and workbooks fast for copyrights. We had learned our lessons about giving our material away when one huge charity asked us for our material, promising a grant, Instead, we heard a couple of years later they had built their own VERY similar project, except theirs charged for services, ours were FREE, and theirs was just for a small group, ours was training veterans and others to spread the programs as fast as they could.. They got a Nobel Peace prize. We keep saying we are not bitter, we keep saying we did not do our work to get awards, or thousands of dollars of grants....but, it hurts. Especially when lied to and that group STILL sends people to US for help when they can not meet the needs, or the veterans and family can not afford their "charitable" services. One other group had the nerve to send us a Cease and Desist using our own name. We said go ahead and sue, we have proof of legal use of this name for decades. That man had the conscience to apologize, his program was not even FOR veterans or first responders, or their families, nor high risk kids. But we learned. Sometimes life is very unfair.

We got sued again later for the same issue. We settled out of Court as our programs were just restarting and one of the veterans said, let's just change that part of the name and keep on training veterans to run their own programs. Smart young man.

Book List:

DRAGON KITES and other stories:

The Grandparents Story list will add 12 new titles this year. We encourage every family to write their own historic stories. That strange old Aunt who when you listen to her stories left a rich and well regulated life in the Eastern New York coastal fashionable families to learn Telegraph messaging and go out to the old west to LIVE her life. That old Grandfather or Grandmother who was sent by family in other countries torn by war to pick up those "dollars in the streets" as noted in the book of that title.

Books in publication, or out by summer 2021

Carousel Horse: A Children's book about equine therapy and what schools MIGHT be and are in special private programs.

Carousel Horse: A smaller version of the original Carousel Horse, both contain the workbooks and the screenplays used for on site stable programs as well as lock down programs where the children and teens are not able to go out to the stables.

Spirit Horse II: This is the work book for training veterans and others interested in starting their own Equine Therapy based programs. To be used as primary education sites, or for supplementing public or private school programs. One major goal of this book is to copyright our founding material, as we gave it away freely to those who said they wanted to help us get grants. They did not. Instead they built their own programs, with grant money, and with donations in small, beautiful stables and won....a Nobel Peace Prize for programs we invented. We learned our lessons, although we do not do our work for awards, or grants, we DO not like to be ripped off, so now we copyright.

Reassessing and Restructuring Public Agencies; This book is an over view of our government systems and how they were expected to be utilized for public betterment. This is a Fourth Grade level condemnation of a PhD dissertation that was not accepted be because the mentor thought it was "against government" .. The first paragraph noted that a request had been made, and referrals given by the then White House.

Reassessing and Restructuring Public Agencies; TWO. This book is a suggestive and creative work to give THE PEOPLE the idea of taking back their government and making the money spent and the agencies running SERVE the PEOPLE ;not politicians. This is NOT against government, it is about the DUTY of the PEOPLE to oversee and control government before it overcomes us.

Could This Be Magic? A Very Short Book. This is a very short book of pictures and the author's personal experiences as the Hall of Fame band VAN HALEN practiced in her garage. The pictures are taken by the author, and her then five year old son. People wanted copies of the pictures, and permission was given to publish them to raise money for treatment and long term Veteran homes.

Carousel TWO: Equine therapy for Veterans. publication pending 2021

Carousel THREE: Still Spinning: Special Equine therapy for women veterans and single mothers. This book includes TWELVE STEPS BACK FROM BETRAYAL for soldiers who have been sexually assaulted in the active duty military and help from each other to heal, no matter how horrible the situation. publication pending 2021

LEGAL ETHICS: AN OXYMORON. A book to give to lawyers and judges you feel have not gotten the justice of American Constitution based law (Politicians are great persons to gift with this book). Publication late 2021

PARENTS CAN LIVE and raise great kids.

Included in this book are excerpts from our workbooks from KIDS ANONYMOUS and KIDS JR, and A PARENTS PLAIN RAP (to teach sexuality and relationships to their children. This program came from a copyrighted project thirty years ago, which has been networked into our other programs. This is our training work book. We asked AA what we had to do to become a real Twelve Step program as this is considered a quasi twelve step program children and teens can use to heal BEFORE becoming involved in drugs, sexual addiction, sexual trafficking and relationship woes, as well as unwanted, neglected and abused or having children murdered by parents not able to deal with the reality of parenting. Many of our original students were children of abuse and neglect, no matter how wealthy. Often the neglect was by society itself when children lost parents to illness, accidents or addiction. We were told, send us a copy and make sure you call it quasi. The Teens in the first programs when surveyed for the outcome research reports said, WE NEEDED THIS EARLIER. SO they helped younger children invent KIDS JR. Will be republished in 2021 as a documentary of the work and success of these projects.

Addicted To Dick. This is a quasi Twelve Step program for women in domestic violence programs mandated by Courts due to repeated incidents and danger, or actual injury or death of their children.

Addicted to Dick 2018 This book is a specially requested workbook for women in custody, or out on probation for abuse to their children, either by themselves or their sexual partners or spouses. The estimated national number for children at risk at the time of request was three million across the nation. During Covid it is estimated that number has risen. Homelessness and undocumented families that are unlikely to be reported or found are creating discussion of a much larger number of children maimed or killed in these domestic violence crimes. THE most important point in this book is to force every local school district to train teachers, and all staff to recognize children at risk, and to report their family for HELP, not punishment. The second most important part is to teach every child on American soil to know to ask for help, no matter that parents, or other relatives or known adults, or unknown adults have threatened to kill them for "telling". Most, if not all paramedics, emergency rooms, and police and fire stations are trained to protect the children and teens, and get help for the family.. PUNISHMENT is not the goal, eliminating childhood abuse and injury or death at the hands of family is the goal of all these projects. In some areas JUDGES of child and family courts were taking training and teaching programs themselves to HELP. FREE..

Addicted to Locker Room BS. This book is about MEN who are addicted to the lies told in locker rooms and bars. During volunteer work at just one of several huge juvenile lock downs, where juveniles who have been convicted as adults, but are waiting for their 18th birthday to be sent to adult prisons, we noticed that the young boys and teens had "big" ideas of themselves, learned in locker rooms and back alleys. Hundreds of these young boys would march, monotonously around the enclosures, their lives over. often facing long term adult prison sentences.

The girls, we noticed that the girls, for the most part were smart, had done well in school, then "something" happened. During the years involved in this volunteer work I saw only ONE young girl who was so mentally ill I felt she was not reachable, and should be in a locked down mental health facility for help; if at all possible, and if teachers, and others had been properly trained, helped BEFORE she gotten to that place, lost in the horror and broken of her childhood and early teen years.

We noticed that many of the young women in non military sexual assault healing programs were "betrayed" in many ways, by step fathers, boyfriends, even fathers, and mothers by either molestation by family members, or allowing family members or friends of parents to molest these young women, often as small children. We asked military sexually assaulted young women to begin to volunteer to help in the programs to heal the young girls and teens, it helped heal them all.

There was NOTHING for the boys that even began to reach them until our research began on the locker room BS theory of life destruction and possible salvaging by the boys themselves, and men in prisons who helped put together something they thought they MIGHT have heard before they ended up in prison.

Americans CAN Live Happily Ever After. Parents edition. One

Americans CAN Live Happily Ever After. Children's edition Two.

Americans CAN Live Happily Ever After. Three. After Covid. This book includes "Welcome to America" a requested consult workbook for children and youth finding themselves in cages, auditoriums on cots, or in foster group homes or foster care of relatives or non-relatives with NO guidelines for their particular issues. WE ASKED the kids, and they helped us write this fourth grade level workbook portion of this book to help one another and each other. Written in a hurry! We were asked to use our expertise in other youth programs, and our years of experience teaching and working in high risk youth programs to find something to help.

REZ CHEESE Written by a Native American /WASP mix woman. Using food, and thoughts on not getting THE DIABETES, stories are included of a childhood between two worlds.

REZ CHEESE TWO A continuation of the stress on THE DIABETES needing treatment and health care from birth as well as recipes, and stories from Native America, including thoughts on asking youth to help stop the overwhelming numbers of suicide by our people.

BIG LIZ: LEADER OF THE GANG Stories of unique Racial Tension and Gang Abatement projects created when gangs and racial problems began to make schools unsafe for our children.

DOLLARS IN THE STREETS, ghost edited for author Lydia Caceras, the first woman horse trainer at Belmont Park.

95 YEARS of TEACHING:

A book on teaching, as opposed to kid flipping

Two teachers who have created and implemented systems for private and public education a combined 95 plus years of teaching talk about experiences and realities and how parents can get involved in education for their children. Included are excerpts from our KIDS ANONYMOUS and KIDS JR workbooks of over 30 years of free youth programs.

A HORSE IS NOT A BICYCLE. A book about pet ownership and how to prepare your children for responsible pet ownership and along the way to be responsible parents. NO ONE needs to own a pet, or have a child, but if they make that choice, the animal, or child deserves a solid, caring forever home.

OLD MAN THINGS and MARE'S TALES. this is a fun book about old horse trainers I met along the way. My husband used to call the old man stories "old man things", which are those enchanting and often very effective methods of horse, pet, and even child rearing. I always said I brought up my children and my students the same as I had trained horses and dogs......I meant that horses and dogs had taught me a lot of sensible, humane ways to bring up an individual, caring, and dream realizing adult who was HAPPY and loved.

STOP TALKING, DO IT

ALL of us have dreams, intentions, make promises. This book is a workbook from one of our programs to help a person make their dreams come true, to build their intentions into goals, and realities, and to keep their promises. One story from this book, that inspired the concept is a high school kid, now in his sixties, that was in a special ed program for drug abuse and not doing well in school. When asked, he said his problem was that his parents would not allow him to buy a motorcycle. He admitted that he did not have money to buy one, insure one, take proper driver's education and licensing examinations to own one, even though he had a job. He was asked to figure out how much money he was spending on drugs. Wasting his own money, stealing from his parents and other relatives, and then to figure out, if he saved his own money, did some side jobs for neighbors and family until he was 18, he COULD afford the motorcycle and all it required to legally own one. In fact, he did all, but decided to spend the money on college instead of the motorcycle when he graduated from high school. His priorities had changed as he learned about responsible motorcycle ownership and risk doing the assignments needed for his special ed program. He also gave up drugs, since his stated reason was he could not have a motorcycle, and that was no longer true, he COULD have a motorcycle, just had to buy it himself, not just expect his parents to give it to him.

Printed in the United States
by Baker & Taylor Publisher Services